The heart-traveller

6

Sri Chinmoy

Songs of the Soul

Ganapati Press

© 2023 SRI CHINMOY CENTRE

ISBN 978-1-911319-50-4

Cover drawing: Soul-Bird by C.K.G.

FIRST EDITION WENT TO PRESS ON 27 August 2023

Songs of the Soul

I — Songs of the Soul

1. Man immortalised

To perfect our human life, by far the greatest necessity is our soul's delight. When we live in the physical, the teeming clouds of desire are natural, necessary and inevitable. When we live in the soul, the ever-mounting flames of aspiration are natural, necessary and inevitable.

When we live in the soul, we spontaneously cultivate God. His Peace, Bliss and Power become ours, absolutely ours. We grow into our spiritual perfection. This perfection is at once our divine heritage in a human body and our unearthly birthright on earthly soil.

The human in us must live under the sheltering wings of the soul. The divine in us must fly and fly into the Beyond with the flying wings of the soul. The human in us must eventually need transformation. The divine in us must eventually need manifestation.

We expect everything from God. It is

supremely good and perfectly reasonable, for who else can fulfil us, both in Heaven and on earth? God is our Face within; God is our Smile without.

God determines everything in us, through us and for us. He is utterly unconditional and infinitely self-giving. Him we serve. Our self-dedicated service unveils Him.

Man's achievement is a supremely unparalleled miracle.

God's achievement is the marriage of His Infinite with His finite.

Lo, God unveiled, man immortalised!

2. Will

Will is myself. Will is my Self. My will is absolutely God's and God's alone.

As my inner Will is, in the world of realisation, so is my outer life, in the world of manifestation.

To my mind's doubt, nothing is real. To my heart's will, everything is real. To conquer my doubts is to grow into the breath of my Will.

I am not afraid of my emotions and frustrations. My emotions and frustrations live in my surrendered Will to God, and will always rejoice in His adamantine Will.

When my inner Will energises my outer existence, all my imponderable troubles and excruciating pangs dissolve into thin air.

Doubt wants to blight my mind.
Fear wants to kill my heart.
Ignorance wants to veil my soul.
Aspiration wants to illumine my life.
Surrender wants to fulfil my life.
Will wants to immortalise my life.

My earthly Will has always a beginning and

an end. My Heavenly Will has no beginning and no end. It has always been and will always be the same. My Will is Eternity's Abode of Truth, built on the rock of God's Vision-in-Reality and God's Reality-in-Vision.

3. My Soul

O soul, I am your body. I am thirty-six years old today. I wish to learn from you.

"Do good."

O Soul, I am your vital. I am nineteen years old. I want to learn from you.

"Be good."

O Soul, I am your mind. I am sixty years old. I need to learn from you.

"See good."

O Soul, I am your heart. I am four years old. Please tell me the secret.

"Remain good."

O Soul, your body again. What do you do with your boundless love?

"I distribute my boundless love to ever-expanding horizons."

O Soul, your vital again. What do you do with your infinite peace?

"I feed the teeming vasts of the past, present and future with my infinite peace."

O Soul, your mind again. What do you do with your vision of the ever-transcending Beyond?

"I feather the golden nest of my Reality's

Infinitude with my vision of the ever-transcending Beyond."

O Soul, once more your heart. Tell me your absolute secret, please.

"I live for the Supreme and for the Supreme alone. This is my absolute secret."

4. My body

O my body, you are a gift of the Supreme. Potentiality inexhaustible you have, deep within you. To misunderstand you means to misunderstand the chosen instrument of God.

You want not, you must not, you cannot conquer the length and breadth of the world with your physical strength. Offer your growing heart to the hearts far and near. Offer your glowing soul to the souls around, below, above. Then alone you become the conqueror and possessor of God's entire universe.

O my body, invoke your soul always for you to lead. Invoke! Never shall the monotony of the uneventful life plague you. With lightning speed yours shall be the ceaseless march... upward to the highest, inward to the inmost, forward to the farthest.

Sing, sing the song of Bliss in Immortality! Breathe, breathe in the breath of Consciousness in Immortality! Live, live the life of Existence in Immortality!

Death? Die you must not. For your death will be a great loss to humanity and by far a greater loss to Divinity. Fight, O my body, fight with ignorance to the bitterest end. Never allow ignorance to envelop you, your outer cloak. Your tearing efforts shall be crowned with success.

O body of mine, fare you well for eternity. May each earthly year of yours have a trillion fulfilling years.

God the Eternal Dreamer is dreaming through you, with you. God the Eternal Reality is living for you, with you and in you.

5. My vital

O my vital, my first choice falls on you. Without your dynamic and stupendous inner urge, nothing can be embodied, nothing can be revealed here on earth.

O my vital, when you fall fast asleep, my mind's undying frustration grips my outer existence. My body's helpless surrender to the Prince of Gloom poisons my inner existence.

Man's most powerful imagination fails to fathom you, your depth. Man's far-flung, brightest wisdom fails to determine you, your breadth.

Yours is the indomitable courage that springs from the fountain of boundless emotion. Kill not your emotion, never. Emotion killed within, fulfilment starved without. Emotion divinely fed within, God the Eternal Delight revealed without.

O my vital, you know no tomorrow. You want to be born, you want to grow and fulfil yourself in the immediacy of today. With the infinite Blessings of the Supreme, on you march across the path of Infinity's bloom, Eternity's glow and

Immortality's lustre.

Your life is green, the ever-aspiring and ever-growing green. Your breath is blue, the ever-encompassing and ever-transforming blue.

O vital of mine, in you is humanity's glowing Hope. With you is Divinity's reverberating Clarion.

6. My mind

O my mind, no earthly chain can fetter you. You are always on the wing. No human thought can control you. You are forever on the move.

O my mind, hard is it for you to believe in my soul's constant fulfilment. And hard is it for me to believe that you are doomed to be the eternal victim of venomous doubts. Alas! You have forgotten. You have forgotten the golden secret: "To remain in the Silence-Room is to open the Fulfilment-Door."

O my mind, vast are your responsibilities. You have to please your superiors: the heart and the soul. Only with your warmest admiration will you be able to conquer the heart. Only with your deepest faith will you be able to conquer the soul. You have also to satisfy your subordinates: the body and the vital. Only with your pure concern will you be able to make the body smile. Only with your genuine encouragement will you be able to help the vital run unmistakably towards good and not pleasure.

O my mind, I need you desperately, either to abide in you or to go beyond you. You see and thus protect the physical in me. You serve and thus reveal the spiritual beyond me.

O my mind, cast aside your long-treasured arid reason. Welcome the ever-virgin faith. Possess the naked sword of conscience. Far above the storms of fear you are destined to climb. Stay no more in self-created sombre shadows of death. Don the golden robes of simplicity, sincerity and purity. Permit not the gales of disbelief to extinguish your inner mounting flame. Yours is the arrow of concentration. Yours is the soil of lightning intuition. Yours is the unhorizoned peace.

Behold the Supreme! He crowns you, O mind of mine, with the laurel of His infinite Bounty.

7. My heart

O my heart, I am divinely proud of you. You do not have the shameful and shameless disease – worry! Never do you drink the deadly venom – doubt! Nothing can be simpler than your pure longings. Nothing can be more spontaneous than your glowing feelings. Nothing can be more fulfilling than your selfless love. Nothing has a more immediate access to the Supreme than your inmost cry.

O my heart, your heavenly day within an earthly day is for God-realisation. Your immortalising minute within a fleeting minute is for God-embodiment. Your revealing second within a vanishing second is for God-manifestation.

O my heart, the other members of the family are afraid of God. You are never! Their lightless, persistent fear is a lifeless, persistent paralysis. In life's journey, others make their own choice. God makes the choice for you. They want to save humanity with their ego's darkest night. You wish to serve humanity with your dedication's brightest day. Their victory is the victory over humanity. Your victory is the victory over yourself.

O my heart, O heart of mine, you are my lifeboat. You sail the uncharted seas of ignorance and reach the Golden Shore of the Beyond.

I am not alone, O my heart. I am with your soaring aspiration. You are not alone. In you and for you is my life's unreserved breath.

Yours is the unfaltering will and unfailing faith in the Supreme. Each petal of the radiant lotus deep within you is perpetually bathed in nectar-rays of the Transcendental Delight.

O sweet, sweeter, sweetest heart of mine, you are not only God's. God also is yours.

8. Man and God

Man forgets. God forgives. Man forgets God's Truth. God forgives man's ignorance.

Man soars. God grows. Man soars in God. God grows in man.

Man loves love. Because he does not have it. God loves love. Because He is all Love.

Man aspires. God inspires. Man aspires. Lo, God descends. God inspires. Lo, man ascends.

Man cries. God's compassion flies to touch man's heart. God cries. Man supplies the message: "It is too early. Wait, you have to wait."

Man is always late in praying and accepting. God is never late in listening and granting. To converse with God, man has his throbbing prayer. God has His illumining Bliss to converse with man. To commune with God, man has his silent meditation. God has His urgent Peace to commune with man.

Absolute Freedom is not a human achievement. It is a blessing of God. Darkest bondage is not a divine achievement. It is an offering of man.

Man wants to know himself and free himself.

God wants to reveal Himself and manifest Himself. Man wants to discover Heaven in the highest plane of consciousness. God wants to uncover Heaven here on earth and nowhere else.

God gives to man what He has and what He is – Love, Joy, Peace, Bliss and Power. Man gives to God what he has not and what he is not – promise! Human promise! Human promise to God for God!

9. War and peace

Man invents war. Man discovers peace. He invents war from without. He discovers peace from within. War man throws. Peace man sows. The smile of war is the flood of human blood. The smile of peace is the love, below, above.

Peace is the whole truth that wishes to enrapture humanity. War is the whole falsehood that wants to capture humanity. Peace begins in the soul and ends in the heart. War begins in the mind and ends in the body.

War forgets peace. Peace forgives war. War is the death of the life human. Peace is the birth of the Life Divine. Our vital passions want war. Our psychic emotions desire peace.

War is clear futility in dire spear-stupidity. Peace is flowing Infinity in glowing Eternity.

Man seeks war when he thinks that the world is not his. Man invites war when he feels that he can conquer the world. Man proclaims war when he dreams that the world has already surrendered to him.

Man seeks peace because his earthly existence desperately needs it. Man welcomes peace because he feels that in peace alone is his life of achievement and fulfilment. Man spreads peace because he wants to transcend death.

The animal in man wars against peace in the outer world, in the world of conflicting ideas. The divine in man wars against ignorance in the inner world, in the world of mounting ideals.

The animal in man wants war for the sake of war, war to devour the snoring world. The divine in man wants peace for the sake of peace, peace to feed the hungry world.

10. My human pride and my pride divine

My human pride feels that I can do everything. My divine pride, the pride that has surrendered itself to the Will of God, knows that I can do everything only when I am inspired, guided, and helped by the Supreme.

My human pride wants the world to understand me, my love, my help and sacrifice. My divine pride, which is the feeling of oneness with all in God, does not wish the world to understand my selfless activities. It feels that if God understands me, knows my motives, then there can be no greater reward.

My human pride drinks the hot water of life – sufferings, struggles and doubts – without a spoon. The result is that my tongue gets badly burnt. My divine pride drinks the same hot water, nay, infinitely more in quantity, but it uses a spoon to drink with, so I suffer not. This spoon is the spoon of liberation, freed from the shackles of ignorance.

My human pride is afraid of saying and ashamed of doing many things. My divine pride is not afraid of saying anything and not ashamed of doing anything, for it knows that God is at once the Doer and the action. Whom am I to be afraid of? What am I to be ashamed of?

My human pride crushes humanity with man-acquired power. My divine pride liberates humanity with God-given Power.

When I say that God is mine and I can use Him at my sweet will, I harbour my human pride. But when I say that I am God's, and my very existence is at His Behest and at His Feet, I cherish Divine pride.

To my human pride, the material world says, "We shall either succeed or we shall fail and perish." To my divine pride, the spiritual world says, "Together shall we endeavour, together shall we succeed."

11. My silence

My silence bridges the gulf between my life's success and my life's failure. My silence does not magnify my defects. Nor does it connive at them. My silence transforms my defects into strength indomitable.

My silence is a climbing flame that warms my world of despair. My silence is my inner light. No problem of mine can defy solution. My silence is a selfless distributor of joy to ever-widening horizons.

In my silence I become a man of sterling character, a prolific writer, a voracious reader, a divine lover, a profound inspirer and a triumphant liberator.

In my deep silence I never become a victim to ignorance, the greatest calamity that can befall any human being. In my growing silence I am convinced that even as a man on this earth, I shall be able to reach heights transcendental, divine.

My glowing silence alone can accelerate my Godward march.

My spreading silence makes me see, feel and

possess satisfaction, unalloyed satisfaction. No more have I to let loose a tirade of tenebrous dissatisfaction.

In activity and vitality I proudly and wrongly feel that I shall have to take care of the whole world. In the heart of silence I humbly and unmistakably realise that it is the Divinity within the world that took care, takes care and shall for ever take care of the entire world.

Silence is my unceasing petition. Silence is my unreserved preparation. Silence is my unlimited realisation. Silence is the unfathomable fount of my life here on earth, there in Heaven.

What God's Silence is... is the eternal Truth. What God's Silence serves is the eternal Purpose. What God's Silence becomes is the inevitable Fulfilment.

12. My love of light

My love of light is my spiritual will. Within it is the power infinite. I give fear no place in my life. My love of light is God's Smile of satisfaction. God's supreme Love manifests in me and through me to transform my human problems into my divine opportunities.

My animal human love is my unnatural experience and uncertain possibility. My divine human love is my natural experience and certain inevitability of my living in the Eternal Now.

My love throbbingly says: "God is all Blessing."

God's Love smilingly says: "My child is all gratitude."

Love radiates the life of harmony, brightens the joy consciousness and sharpens the sword of intuition. Love is always ready to meet man's every soulful demand. Love conquers all that is unlike God. It is, indeed, supreme over all.

Love gives me my importance in the cosmic Vision of God. Nobody remembers me save my love. My sole treasure is love. Love's treasure is

God's Heart.

Love is the undeniable truth of my identity as God's son, chosen son. Love is the unique combination of Heaven's freedom and earth's discipline. In Heaven's freedom is earth's emancipation. In earth's discipline is Heaven's manifestation.

No time-born desire can rend my love of light. My love of light flies beyond the widespread net of death. Mine is the love that has the birthless origin and the deathless end.

13. Self-sacrifice

A human being has many divine qualities. But there has never been another unparalleled divine quality like man's self-sacrifice, nor can there ever be. God's own soulful Message to humanity in all walks of life is self-sacrifice. The brightest self-sacrifice can easily ease and diminish the darkest trials and stresses of human life.

He who is all sacrifice can never go through life as a failure. His is the perpetual victory. His is the spontaneous inner joy. What is to be sacrificed? One's life-breath. How to sacrifice? With the feeling of universal oneness.

To despair's invitation, self-sacrifice says No. To delight's invitation, self-sacrifice says Yes.

God secretly blesses me from Heaven when I wish to grow into sacrifice. God openly blesses me on earth when my earthly existence becomes all sacrifice.

Man's choice is joy. Joy's choice is sacrifice. Sacrifice's choice is nothing. This nothing is verily the unfoldment of everything, and the fulfilment of man and God.

A man of no sacrifice wants to possess the world with his strongest might. A man of sacrifice wishes to be possessed by the world with his all-surrendering right. To love life is to sacrifice our divinity within. To sacrifice life is to transform our humanity without.

When I sacrifice my material possessions, I see God coming smilingly towards me. When I sacrifice my austerities, I see God marching dynamically towards me. When I sacrifice my spiritual achievements, I see God running speedily towards me.

14. Love, devotion, surrender

Love is action. Devotion is practice. Surrender is experience.

Love is realisation. Devotion is revelation. Surrender is manifestation.

Love is the meaning of life. Devotion is the secret of life. Surrender is the Goal of life.

In my love, I see God the Mother. In my devotion, I see God the Father. In my surrender, I see God the Mother and God the Father together in one body.

Love without devotion is absurdity. Devotion without surrender is futility.

Love with devotion was my journey's start. Devotion with surrender is my journey's close.

I love the Supreme because I came from Him. I devote myself to the Supreme because I wish to go back to Him. I surrender myself to the Supreme because He lives in me and I in Him.

15. *There was a time*

There was a time when I prayed to God for all the things I wanted. God heard me and gave me a soulful cry.

There was a time when I prayed to God for all the things I needed. My God heard me and gave me a soulful smile.

There was a time when I prayed to God only for the Truth. He heard me and gave me a soulful embrace.

There was a time when I prayed to God neither for realisation nor for liberation, neither for Infinity nor for Eternity, but for the Fulfilment of His own Will. My God heard me and gave me His Breath.

There was a time when God wanted me to be His Desire.

I touched His Feet and I became.

There was a time when God wanted me to be His Aspiration.

I touched His Heart and I became.

There was a time when God wanted me to be His Realisation.

I touched His Soul and I became.

There was a time when God wanted me to be nothing but Reality.
I touched His Dream-Boat and I became.

16. *My acceptance of God and God's acceptance of me*

Away with my halting and doubting mind! My implicit acceptance of God will invariably be able to meet the teeming needs of my aspiring soul.

Him I have accepted, my God, the Lord Supreme. No more can my world fall. My age-old fear's torture is now being transformed into my heart's rapture. How? Just by virtue of my purest acceptance of God.

Happy I was because He implanted in me His Message of Hope. Happier I am because He is shaping me into His own Image. Happiest shall I be because He will awaken in me His Eternity and reveal through me His Infinity and fulfil me with His Immortality.

Perfect I am not, far from it. I make Himalayan blunders day in, day out. But my sweet Lord is neither severe nor unforgiving. Stern Justice He is not. All Compassion He always is.

God has accepted me. Something more. He has assumed my human nature so that He can be fully conscious of my wants and needs. He is freeing me from the world marred with ignorance. He is freeing me from the life eclipsed by the shadow of ruthless death.

My earth is linked with His Heaven through my loving surrender and His unconditional Concern. Through my personal effort I can never better myself; it is like trying to straighten the tail of a dog for good. I have come to God just as I am. I know that what I do not consciously overcome will mercilessly overcome me. But my Lord out of His infinite Bounty says that He will overcome it, the wildest ignorance, in me and for me.

In my acceptance of God I have to give up all that would separate me from Him. In His acceptance of me, He has given me a new world and His Breath entire.

17. God's Will and my will

When God's Will is my will, I have not to give up anything, for He is with everything and in everything. When I act contrary to God's Will, I injure my body, torture my life and encage my soul-bird. When I am in perfect slavery to venomous doubts, my will becomes empty of God's Will. When I am absolutely obedient to the Truth's inevitability, I grow into God's adamantine Will. When I live the life of faith, God's Will transforms my earthly dreams into Heavenly visions. When I live the life of proud self-assertion, God's Will forgets me, earth hates me and Heaven disowns me.

I encircle the Supreme in the arms of my utter helplessness. He encircles me in the arms of His all-sheltering Protection. I squander His Blessings and Compassion. He grows His Hope in me and feeds His Promise to me.

My will is the opening of my aspiring heart to the Supreme. I meditate, not because I want Him to know that I meditate on Him, but because I want to enable myself to receive Him in infinite measure. During my meditation, when I swim in the sea of love and devotion, He comes down to me. During my meditation, when the sun of wisdom and peace dawns within me, He lifts me up to Him.

I silently pray. He secretly hears. My heart's mounting flame rises up and touches the Throne of His Compassion.

The Supreme never demands my belief in Him before He has given me evidence, infinitely more than necessary, upon which I can found my implicit faith. If I want to doubt Him, He has given me abundant opportunity to do so. Verily, here lies the magnanimity of His Compassion-Light for me.

My will and God's Will. When my will is approved by God's Will, my pure heart does not have an abiding inner bliss. But when my heart unreservedly and soulfully obeys God's Will and I accept it as my own will, infinite joy grows within my heart and eternal joy flows through my heart.

18. My and I

I have infinite opportunities to go to God. I have unthinkable possibilities to go to the King of Ignorance.

When I live in material realities, I am a natural human being. When I live in spiritual realities, I am a supernatural divine being.

I possess and I am possessed by a fast-moving world. Although I myself am a colossal problem, I can solve considerably the countless problems of the world. How? Just by becoming a faithful servant to God's Will and by surrendering my expectations to God's guidance and assurance.

My fear of God is a roadblock to my life's peace. My love for God is a foretaste of the joy of God's cosmic creation.

To achieve my Goal was difficult. I have done it. To maintain my Goal is more difficult. I do it. To become my Goal will be most difficult. I shall do it, and I shall do it with my heart's mounting cry, with my soul's searching light, with my mind's sublime silence, with the forceful dynamism of my vital and finally with my body's absolute surrender.

I pray to God to transform my life into one long effort, fearless and egoless, so that I can derive the most fulfilling achievements from the most unpromising situations.

Every second is an open door to unparalleled opportunities. Let me be long on Heavenly performance and short on earthly talk.

I not only have a soul. I am the soul. I am not the ego. Neither do I need one. He that is not with me in my soul's endeavour is against me. But I must know that my God is also his God. No compromise, no compromise with the world's threatening Night and unaspiring Day.

19. Patience

What is patience? It is a divine virtue. Unfortunately, we are not only badly wanting in this divine virtue, but we also neglect it most foolishly.

What is patience? It is an inner assurance of God's unreserved Love and unconditional Guidance. Patience is God's Power hidden in us to weather the teeming storms of life.

If failure has the strength to turn your life into bitterness itself, then patience has the strength to turn your life into the sweetest joy. Do not surrender to fate after a single failure. Failure, at most, precedes success. But success once achieved, confidence becomes your name.

Have patience in the body; you will be able to accept the whole world. Have patience in the vital; you will be able to hold the whole world. Have patience in the mind; you will neither forget nor lose the world. Have patience in the heart; you will feel that the world is not only with you and in you, but for you.

Time is a flying bird. Do you want to capture the bird and encage it? Your fondest dreams will be transformed into fruitful realities if you just know the secret of growing the patience-tree in your heart.

Patience is your sincere surrender to God's Will. This surrender is by no means the effacement of the finite self which you now are, but a total transcendence of your finite existence to the Infinite Self.

In silence patience speaks to you: "Try to live the inner life. You will not only see and reach your Goal, but also become the Goal."

Patience can never be imposed on you from outside. It is your own inner wealth, wisdom, peace and victory.

20. Joy

Joy is the inner light that illumines my darkest night.

When I am in Joy, God feeds me. And I feed God only when I share my Joy with others.

When I have inner Joy, I will always be blessed with an abundance of spontaneity and creativity.

When I look up with Joy, I will have God as my Employer.

When I look around with Joy, I will have God as my Supervisor.

When I look forward with Joy, I will have God as my Paymaster.

Joy is my dynamic oneness with the Supreme. Since my soul is integrally one with the Supreme, there is no challenge too great for me. Absolutely none.

My Joy is my established faith in the Supreme. Unlike others who do not have faith in the Supreme, I do not think and feel that I am always wrong, meaningless and useless. To be sure, those who are wanting in faith are the victims of frustration. To them, life is a barren desert, God is a colossal daydream, death is a roaring lion right in front of them.

Before my heart's Joy calls upon God, His omnipotent Grace will answer. It is a true truth.

To try to explain Joy is to fail always. Because it is dubious. To try to taste Joy is to succeed always. Because it is obvious.

Joy is the peace embodied. Joy is the power revealed. The embodied peace is the masculine aspect of the Divine. The revealed power is the feminine aspect of the Divine.

My heart's Joy fathoms the Deepest. My mind's Joy reaches the Farthest. My soul's Joy achieves the Highest.

21. Emotion

Emotion is a gift of God. It fills our days with loving thoughts and glowing deeds. Owing to our confused thinking, we misuse emotion. Emotion is the dynamic fulness of Completion.

Emotion tells us that the ever-increasing life-energy is constantly flowing through us, renewing and revitalising our inner being. Emotion not only sweetens and intensifies our life, it also awakens our outer life to experience perfection in every field of manifestation.

In emotion there is a creative urge. This urge is eternal. The creative urge finally has to enter into the God-ideal which is Immortality embodied and Perfection revealed.

Emotion has an inner perception of the divine Unity. The knowledge of the intellect secretly loves emotion. The understanding of the mind silently loves emotion. The wisdom of the heart openly and soulfully loves emotion.

We must endeavour to uncover within ourselves the deepest depth of emotion so that we can become the widest channels for the divine expression of Beauty, Joy, Power and

Truth.

Emotion is not the confusion of experience. It is the reality that grows in perfection.

When inspiration and aspiration are supported by our psychic emotion, we come into conscious contact with the Supreme. The perfect Reality then prevails in and through our outer existence.

Emotion is not the victim of frustration. Emotion is no demonstration. It is the inner spontaneous joy through which we express ourselves in the world we live in.

The psychic emotion is the Fountain of Abundance. And with this Fountain we enter into the world of revealing thought, fulfilling action and transforming realisation.

22. Is the world an illusion?

The world is not an illusion. True illusion can never be comprehensible, whereas the world is easily comprehensible when we go deep within and look at it with our inner eye. It is the illusion that is unreal and not the world of ours.

As my body is real, even so is my God's Body, the world.

Nothing comes out of an empty void. God has projected the universe out of His Existence-Consciousness-Bliss. He has created the world. He has become the world. He wills and He becomes. He smilingly unveils without what He is silently within.

23. *God gave me but I have lost*

God gave me Joy. But I have lost it. I have lost it because I have made friends with suffering, consciously and wholeheartedly, without His approval.

God gave me Peace. But I have lost it. I have lost it because I have welcomed the restless vital horse to carry me to the worlds beyond. This, too, I have done without God's permission.

God gave me Love, His soulful Love. But I have lost it. I have lost it because, in my utter stupidity, I have discovered and embraced human love, to be the goal of my life. This great discovery has been made by me, by me alone. God has not been invoked to participate in my grand discovery.

God gave me the Truth, His highest Truth. But I have lost it. I have given it, God's Truth, to Falsehood unreservedly. Alas! After having greedily accepted God's Truth from me, Falsehood mercilessly hates my stupidity, my helpless ignorance. Now I am all alone. My existence is neither in God nor in Falsehood, but deep inside my roaring self-annihilation.

24. My prayer

My prayer can smile only twice. Once when I silence my outer senses, once when I open the portal of my soul.

My prayer lies in loving God for His own sake. My prayer is the destroyer of errors, born and unborn.

The reality is determined only by one thing: prayer – prayer in its embodiment, prayer in its dynamic operation.

Prayer is best expressed in my day-to-day life when my prayer has become a spontaneous, self-giving surrender to the Will of God.

Seeking is the plane fare in the realm of spirituality. Striving is the ticket. When seeking and striving have played their respective roles, "surrendering" leads me to my seat in the plane.

Eldorado can no longer hide from me when my genuine prayer enables me to see my soul in life and my life in the soul.

Audible prayer is often a self-satisfying solemnity. Silent prayer in lone self-poise is the fulfilment of Eternity.

Prayer is struggle when I want to be an

all-knowing mind. Prayer is nectar when I want to be an all-dedicating life.

They say that prayer is the daughter of suffering. But I say that prayer is the Mother of Delight.

25. Spirituality

A man with no spirituality is a pitiful victim of circumstances. A man with spirituality is God's Smile of victory.

A true seeker is not ridden by anxiety. His future abides in the present. His moments are wedded to constant opportunity. His dictionary does not house the word "postponement". His opportunity transforms itself into reality. His reality transforms itself into practicability.

As a plant cannot live without the sun and air, even so a seeker cannot live without spirituality. Spirituality is his inner urge to achieve absolute Peace, Light and Bliss. Each seeker has a particular temperament of his own, hence his way of spiritual discipline must have its own uniqueness. Confusion and conflict run riot when I invite others to enter into my path or when I myself enter into others' paths.

There are people who cherish the idea that spirituality is no longer alive. A genuine seeker cannot see eye to eye with them. Spirituality has not died, and it can never die, for God has made spirituality as the sole necessity of humanity to enter into His Eternity, Infinity and Immortality. And the same spirituality is also God's necessity to enter into humanity, its stark bondage and wild ignorance.

26. Spirituality and science

Spirituality needs God. It has God. Science has no God. Neither does it need one.

The funniest thing is that science is constantly and perpetually challenged by science itself. The scientific discovery of yore pales into insignificance before the scientific discovery of today, whereas the realisation of Krishna, Buddha and the Christ defy the strength of challenge, outer or inner. It is true that science offers man all his practical needs. It is equally true that spirituality reveals to man the meaning of his life and the significance of his earthly existence.

Science condemns the seeker by accusing him of being afraid of the Unknown. The seeker blesses the utter stupidity of science and calmly says that he is not at all afraid of the Unknown. He is just enamoured of the Unknown and he cannot help embracing the Unknown.

Science depends on outer experiment. Spirituality depends on inner searching and seeking. A scientist discovers the power that very often threatens even his own life. A spiritual seeker discovers the power that guides and moulds his life into a life of divine fulfilment.

Now what should be the relation between science and spirituality? It should be a relation of mutual acceptance and true understanding. It is an act of folly on our part to expect the same truth, the same knowledge and the same power from both science and spirituality. We must not do that. Neither must we set up the same goal for science and spirituality.

Let us listen to the message of Matter through the voice of science. Let us listen to the message of the Spirit through the voice of spirituality. Finally, let us not forget that spirituality is the soul and science is the body.

27. Mother earth and her son

O my Mother-Earth, my usefulness has ended.

O my son, your ignorance has ended.

O my Mother-Earth, I have sung my swan song.

O my son, but you have not sung God's Song and my song.

What are your songs?

My song is aspiration and God's Song is inspiration. If you and I sing the song of aspiration, God will welcome us.

If you and God sing the song of inspiration, I shall welcome both of you.

When I welcome you and God, I know you will offer me your God, your Goal, and from God I shall also get you, His Soul.

When God welcomes us, you and me, I shall give Him the breath of my existence and you will give Him the soul-flames of your liberation.

II — Blossoms of the heart

28. *What is my God doing?*

What is my God doing in Heaven? He is dreaming.
   What is my God doing on Earth? He is struggling.
   In His Dream He is His Goal.
   In His Struggle He is His Soul.
   What is Heaven doing? Heaven is descending with God's Feet of Beauty.
   What is Earth doing? Earth is ascending with God's Eye of Purity.
   What is my God doing to please Heaven?
   He is dancing.
   What is my God doing to please Earth?
   He is crying.
   What else is my God doing? He is carrying me to the Head of His Heaven to show me the embodiment of His highest Height which He is going to share with me unconditionally. He is carrying me into the Heart of His Earth to show

me the embodiment of His deepest Depth which He is going to share with me unconditionally.

29. HERE

H represents humility. Without humility my spirituality is curiosity, my spirituality is futility.

E represents eternity. With faith my spirituality is eternity's wealth, my spirituality is eternity's delight.

R represents revelation. Without devotion to God's self-revelation in me, my life is a breathless hush, my life is the song of death.

E represents evolution. With my surrender's light I am God's ever-blooming and expanding evolution. I become the selfless link between His Infinity and His Immortality, I become His Vision's Reality and His Reality's Vision.

30. NOW

N – No

I needs must say "No" to desire's arrival, "No" to fear's embrace, "No" to doubt's poison, "No" to ignorance's leadership, and "No" to death's reign.

O – Open

I needs must open myself to the smile of the farthest beyond, to the love of the deepest beyond, and to the blessings of the highest beyond.

W – Without and With

Without God's Dream, I was. Now, with His Dream, I am. Without the living, protecting, transforming and immortalising God, I was. That past of mine is buried in oblivion's hush. With me NOW is God's living Breath, His protecting Silence, His transforming Will and His immortalising Delight.

31. God is my personal experience

God is my personal experience. In Him is my life's confidence. With me is His assurance in life and death, and beyond time and space. I live for God. I live to serve Him with my heart's surrender and with my soul's joy. He lives for me. He lives to present me with His all-transcending Vision, to transform my existence into His heavenly Reality.

When I look up into the skies, He is unchangeable. When I look into the world, He is all changing. Backward I look, He is veiled. Forward I look, He is revealed. When I look within, He is never new. When I look without, He is never old.

32. I prayed

I prayed to God for Power. He said, "Take it and use it." I prayed to God for Light. He said, "Take it and spread it." I prayed to God for Peace. He said, "Take it and unveil your divinity." I prayed to God for Bliss. He said, "Take it and stay in your Source." I prayed to God for Love. He said, "Take Me; I am yours."

33. My liberator and my transformer

To know the Truth, I shall have to be conscious of the Supreme. To possess the Truth, I shall have to stay with the Supreme. To become the Truth, I shall have to breathe in the Breath of the Supreme.

How can I serve the Supreme? By practising His Thought. How can I reveal the Supreme? By practising His Will. How can I fulfil the Supreme? By practising His Truth.

My soul's aspiration cries for my Supreme, the Liberator. My life's breath cries for my Supreme, the Transformer.

34. I have loved

I have loved Humanity. Humanity says, "No longer are you a stranger to me."

I have loved Infinity. Infinity says, "No longer are you caught by space."

I have loved Eternity. Eternity says, "No longer will you be caught by time."

I have loved Immortality. Immortality says, "No longer will death be able to bind you."

At long last I have loved God. God says, "My child, from now on, you have bound Me in your divine embrace. You have bound Immortality, Infinity, Eternity and Humanity."

35. *Your best instrument*

My Lord, who is Your best instrument?
Is he the one who thinks of You constantly?
No, he is not. Never.
Is he the one who loves You wholeheartedly?
No, he is not. Never.
Is he the one who devotes himself to You unceasingly?
No, he is not. Never.
Is he the one who surrenders himself to You unconditionally?
No, he is not. Never.
Who, then, is Your best instrument, my Lord?
My best instrument is he who has discovered Me as the Eternally Perfect slave of his desires of yesterday, his aspirations of today and his realisations of tomorrow.

He who thinks of Me constantly enters into My world of adamantine Will.

He who loves Me wholeheartedly enters into My world of transcendental Peace.

He who devotes himself to Me unceasingly enters into My world of unfathomable Ecstasy.

He who surrenders himself to Me unconditionally enters into My world of supreme Fulfilment.

But he who thinks of Me as the eternally Perfect slave of his desires of Yesterday, his aspirations of Today and his realisation of Tomorrow enters into My world of Soul and Goal which is equally his.

36. If it is all true

Beauty tells me that I am ugly.
   Purity tells me that I am impure.
   Sincerity tells me that I am insincere.
   I ask my sweet Lord if it is all true.
   My Lord says, "How can you be ugly, My child, when My own Light is your body? How can you be impure, My child, when My Divinity is your heart's birthright? How can you be insincere, My child, when I, Myself, use your soul to speak through your mouth?"

37. Another God, another man

My God, how old are You?

My child, I shall tell you. But first tell Me how old *you* are.

I am just a year old.

My child, if you are a year old, I am one day younger than you and one day older than you; one day younger than you in imperfection and one day older than you in perfection. Give Me half the imperfection that you have and take from Me half the perfection that I have. Let us be fully equal.

What will happen, my God, if You and I become fully equal?

My child, when we two become fully equal, you will be known as another God and I will be known as another man.

38. When I forget, when I remember

When I forget to think of God once, He smiles.

When I forget to think of God twice, He laughs.

When I forget to think of God thrice, He cries.

He smiles lovingly because I am helpless.

He laughs profoundly because I am hopeless.

He cries sincerely because I am shameless.

When I remember to think of God once, He blesses me.

When I remember to think of God twice, He caresses me.

When I remember to think of God thrice, He embraces me.

He blesses me, my life of aspiration.

He caresses me, my life of realisation.

He embraces me, my life of manifestation.

39. When I discover God

When I discover God in Himself, I see the living, growing and glowing God. When I discover God in me, I see the starving, sleeping and crying God. When I discover God in Himself, He is the Eternal Wonder. When I discover God in me, He is the Eternal Mystery.

I discover God's Infinite Power and cry out: "Give me Your Infinite Power." God says: "It is yours."

God discovers my limitless weakness and cries out: "Give Me your limitless weakness." I say: "No, my wealth, absolutely mine."

God fails, I win. God fails to illumine me. I win to destroy me.

40. I sought and he caught

I sought God's guidance. He caught my fear.

I sought God's Wisdom-light. He caught my Ignorance-night.

I sought God's all-illumining Truth. He caught my all-spreading Falsehood.

I sought God to own Him. He caught me to give Himself.

I sought God because without Him I can do

nothing.

He caught me because without me He wants to do nothing.

I sought God, I am now fulfilled.

God caught me. He is now revealed.

41. God's visiting hours

When I see my God in reason, He is Justice.
When I see my God in faith, He is Protection.
When I see my God in love, He is Compassion.
When I see my God in will, He is Vision.
When I see my God in joy, He is Perfection.
When I see my God in truth, He is Fulfilment.

My breath invokes God throbbingly, my soul silently, my heart lovingly, my mind hesitantly, my vital unconsciously and my body fearfully.

There are two choice hours for my God to visit me. Once when my soulful life is without haste; once when my life's mounting flame is without rest.

42. Is my God complete? Is my God perfect? Is my God fulfilled?

Oh, my God, are You complete?
No, I am not.
Why are You not complete?
Perhaps you are the cause.
Oh, my God, are You perfect?
No, I am not.
Why are You not perfect?
Perhaps you are the cause.
Oh, my God, are You fulfilled?
No, I am not.
Why are You not fulfilled?
Perhaps you are the cause.
My God, You are a very clever God.
You put the entire blame on me.
All right. I accept.
Now, tell me,
How can I make You complete?
How can I make You perfect?
How can I fulfil You?
To make Me complete, my child,

Give Me your heart of heartful love.
To make Me perfect, my child,
Give Me your life of lifeless ignorance.
To fulfil Me, my child,
Give Me your soul of soulful promise.

43. Is it all correct?

The world loves me. I love the world. My Lord loves me and the world. I ask my sweet Lord if it is all correct.

My Lord says: "The world does not love you, my child. The world loves only your appreciation. You do not love the world, my child. You love only the world's admiration. But I love you and the world. You have the capacity to appreciate. The world has the capacity to admire. I have the capacity to perfect. I shall perfect your appreciation by directing it towards Me. I shall perfect the world's admiration by directing it towards Me. Your feeble appreciation divinised by Me will be the bloom of your true love for the world. The world's fruitless admiration transformed by Me will be the bloom of the world's true love for you. In the near future you and the world will love each other the way I love you two – unreservedly and unconditionally."

44. I have seven eyes

I have seven eyes. My two normal eyes tell me what I should see around me. My eye in between the eyebrows – a little above – tells me that what I see in the highest region of consciousness I can eventually become. My eye in my heart tells me that mere seeing the Truth is not enough; I have to feel the Truth as my own and I have to feel myself as its very own. My eyes inside my feet tell me that to see is to believe the past, my past, my backward race. My eye inside the crown of my head tells me that to believe is to see the future, my future, my forward race and my Golden All.

45. My humility

God is my Superior, my only Superior. I am humble to Him. This is my supreme duty. God's children are my equals. I am humble to them. This is my greatest necessity. Pride is my inferior. I am humble to pride. This is my surest safety.

My humility is not self-denial. My humility in silence affirms what I truly have in my world without and what I surely am in my world within.

My humility is not the abstinence from self-love. I love myself. I really do. I love myself because in me the highest Divinity proudly breathes.

Self-conceit tells me that I can easily destroy the world. Self-exploit tells me that the world is at my feet. My humility tells me that I have neither the capacity nor the desire to destroy the world. My humility tells me that the world and I do have the real capacity and the sincere desire to cry for perfect perfection. My humility further tells me that the world is not at my feet, far from it. I carry the world devotedly towards its self-realisation. The world carries me lovingly and openly towards my self-manifestation.

When I am all humility, I neither underestimate nor overestimate my life. What I do is to judge my life exactly, the way my Lord Supreme judges my life.

My soul's owner is Divinity.
My heart's owner is sincerity.
My mind's owner is clarity.
My vital's owner is capacity.
My body's owner is purity.

46. Be happy

Be happy

You will grow into God's greatest blessing, His highest pride.

Be happy

Yesterday's world wants you to enjoy its surrendered breath.

Today's world wants you to enjoy its surrendering breath.

Tomorrow's world wants you to enjoy its fulfilling breath.

Be happy

Be happy in the morning with what you have.

Be happy in the evening with what you are.

Be happy

Don't complain. Who complains? The blind beggar in you.

When you complain, you dance in the mire of ignorance-condition.

When you don't complain, all conditions of the world are at your feet, and God gives you a new name: aspiration.

Aspiration is the supreme wealth in the world of light and delight.

Be happy

Do you want never to be poor? Then be happy. Do you want ever to be great? Then be happy.

Be happy

You will get what you like most. You will be what you like best.

Be happy

When you are happy, you and God command each other.

God commands you lovingly. You command God hastily.

When you are unhappy, the hostile forces command you ruthlessly, doubt commands you openly, bondage commands you triumphantly and fear commands you unconditionally.

Be happy

God sees in you His aspiring Creation, His transforming Realisation, His illumining Revlation and His fulfilling Manifestation.

Be happy

God sees in you another God.
God sees you as another God.
God sees you and He as One.

47. *Ambition*

Ambition. If you cast aside your ambition while still in the unaspiring life, lo, you have become a brainless sheep.

Ambition. Embrace ambition in your aspiring life; lo, you become the condemned convict. You can never come out of the finite.

Ambition. In your outer life, ambition is the highest height.

Ambition. In your inner life, ambition is the darkest night.

Ambition. In your outer life, the closer you come towards the land of fulfilling ambition, the mightier is your hopeful security.

Ambition. In your inner life, the farther away you go from the shore of ambition, the greater is the strength of God's protection for you.

Before you became an aspirant, ambition was the highest aim. After you have become an aspirant, ambition is not only a low aim, but a serious fall.

Be sure, ambition is not aspiration. Ambition wants to command the world. Aspiration cries to serve the Creator in His creation.

Ambition is a human passion, never to be satisfied. Aspiration is a divine glorification, ever to be satisfied.

Ambition is the end of human realisation. Aspiration is the beginning of divine realisation.

Ambition is the chosen child of man. Aspiration is the chosen child of God.

Aspiration. Aspiration. Aspiration. In aspiration an aspirant lives far above the skies. In aspiration an aspirant's eye becomes one with the highest God. In aspiration an aspirant's heart becomes the Absolute.

48. My occupation

My occupation is at once my delightful responsibility and my soulful necessity.

My only responsibility is to fulfil the Will of God. God has given me the love needed to love the world. God has given me the wisdom needed to become the world. God has given me the surrender needed to obey Him in the night of the finite and in the Light of the Infinite.

My only necessity is to fulfil all God's promises to the world. He has made four promises: the perfection of human nature, the extinction of human death, the divinisation of the human body and the manifestation of His own realisation on earth.

My God does not force me to do anything, but He instructs me privately on how to do everything divinely.

My earthly occupation is to be far above the mire of ignorance. My heavenly occupation is to enter into the breath of ignorance and transform its very life.

I want the atmosphere of my outer occupation to be surcharged with God's thoughts. I want the conscience of my inner occupation to be formed by God's influence.

God's secret thirst is the embodiment of my aspiring life's occupation. God's sacred hunger is the realisation of my fulfilling soul's occupation.

My inner occupation is silence. My outer occupation is surrender. In my silence I see God, the Eternal Gift. In my surrender I become God, the Infinite Gift.

I think of God. This is my immortalising duty. God thinks of me. This is His self-chosen duty.

APPENDIX

BIBLIOGRAPHY

Sri Chinmoy:

Songs of the Soul, Herder and Herder, New York, 1971.

Suggested citation key is: SNS

TABLE OF CONTENTS

Songs of the Soul	9
Appendix	69
Bibliography	71
Table of Contents	73

The heart-traveller

1. Aspiration-Flames — Aspiration and God's Hour
2. A Sri Chinmoy primer
3. Everest-Aspiration
4. New Year's Messages from Sri Chinmoy (1966-2007)
5. Flower-Flames
6. Songs of the Soul
7. Eternity's Breath

www.ingramcontent.com/pod-product-compliance
Lightning Source LLC
Chambersburg PA
CBHW030308100526
44590CB00012B/566